# What I Am Always Waiting For
## Selected Poems

# What I Am Always Waiting For
## Selected Poems

Malcolm Miller

with an Introduction by Rod Kessler

GRAYSON BOOKS
West Hartford, Connecticut
www.graysonbooks.com

ISBN: 978-1-7335568-4-2
Library of Congress Control Number: 2020911575

Book & cover design by Cindy Stewart
Cover photo by John Noonan, courtesy of Unsplash.com

# Acknowledgements

Many thanks to the following writers who assisted in reading and selecting poems from among the 3,500 that Malcolm Miller left behind:

Maile Black, Kevin Carey, Carl Carlsen, M.P. Carver,
Felicia M. Connolly, R.G. Evans, Linda Flaherty Haltmaier,
Pamela Harris, Mikko Harvey, Mark Hillringhouse, Elisabeth Weiss,
Claire Keyes, Jacquelyn Malone, Jennifer Martelli, Linda McCarriston,
Dawn Paul, Kayla Russell, Clemens Schoenebeck, J.D. Scrimgeour,
Katherine Towler, Susan G. Tyler, Cindy Veach

Thanks also to *Paterson Literary Review*, where "My Mother Has to Go to the Rehab Hospital" first appeared.

# Contents

## Poems Like This

## Among Human Things

# Introduction

Malcolm Miller (1930-2014), poet of Salem, Massachusetts, and Montreal, wrote sixty-one books of poetry, all but two self-published. His conventionally published collections—books issued in 1969 and 1970 by Tundra Books of Montreal—were lavish, expensive productions interlarded with pages of full-color art. Distressed at having become a coffee-table poet for the well-to-do, Miller thereafter distrusted publishing houses and editors and went his own way,

His self-published works, produced between 1992-2013, were cheaply printed chapbook-sized numbers with gray covers, running 55 to 72 pages. The print shops did little beyond reproducing his typescripts. You could tell when the ribbon on Miller's manual typewriter needed replacing. (For his last ten books, his portable machine broken, his poems were printed in handwritten editions.) He never hesitated to crowd poems on a page. These were not intended for anyone's coffee table.

In the early 1990s, one of these books appeared in my mailbox at the English Department of Salem State College, where I taught creative writing. Inserted in its pages was a handwritten letter inviting me, if I liked the poems, to send $5 to Malcolm Miller, Apt. F, 9 Pioneer Terrace, Salem MA 01970.

The inside cover contained a printed author's note:

Malcolm Miller was born in Salem
Massachusetts, served in the United
States Navy and graduated from
McGill University.

I was an overworked professor with numerous campus responsibilities, and I was also a new father. I barely found time to mark up my students' writing. And in those days—I'll admit it—I held my nose at self-publishing. I never bothered to read this stranger's poems, not one. I didn't even open his book, but I did slip it onto a shelf in my office—and I put a five-dollar bill in the mail.

Months later, another appeared. I shelved it, unread, beside the first one, and sent off five more dollars. After a year or so, it happened again. And again. Eventually I had a dozen of Miller's books.

One day in 2011, after almost twenty years of this, a new one arrived. I opened it, and my life changed. His poems struck me as brilliant, important, original, wry—even accusatory, pressing me to ask myself was I fully alive in my own life?

I wrote to his Pioneer Terrace address (a public housing complex, I would find out, and less than a half-mile from campus) inviting him to meet for coffee. He wrote back: no dice. I wrote again. Would he give a reading on campus? (No) Speak to my poetry-writing class? (No). He wrote that he wished me well with my teaching but that he was "not able to meet in social groups anymore...I am hermit, anchorite, almost leper." Yet when I tried again, asking if we might include his work in the college's literary magazine, he assented.

And so, in September of 2013 I found my way to his building, bringing ten complimentary copies of *Soundings East* with a cover naming Malcolm Miller as its featured poet. The tall, bald, imposing 82-year-old who eventually answered the buzzer was so weak, so breathless, that he needed to rest on the staircase to gather the strength to climb back to his second-floor apartment. (In the months to follow, he seemed sturdier, but he died a year later of congestive heart failure.)

But on that day, amid signs of his penurious life—a ratty sleeping bag on the bare floor, his clothes stuffed into plastic bags hanging off doorknobs, no phone, no television, just the one chair—we began a friendship. He had a piercing, interrogating gaze, but there was humor in his eyes. Was I (like him) a Jew? He spoke of his long-dead wife, a Russian Jew from Montreal whose dark features made her look almost Asian. She was the subject of many of his poems, he said. And what did I think of John Updike's novels? Robinson Jeffers' poetry? He told me of listening outside the opened door of Robert Lowell's class at Harvard in 1970—and then of speaking with Lowell for ten minutes. Was any good poetry being written today?

Perhaps my answers persuaded him, or perhaps my obvious respect for his poetry won his trust. I like to think that he intuited the role I would soon be playing after his death. He gave me more of his self-published books, and a copy of the 1970 oversized coffee-table art-book of his poems, *Emperor of Massachusetts*.

Two more telling details from that day: When asked if he needed money, this apparent pauper retrieved from a kitchen drawer an oversized envelope stuffed with hundred-dollar bills, packets of them, held by rubber bands. He'd saved some $36,000, explaining, "I can't keep it in a bank because the housing authority would find out."

Living the ascetic life was obviously his choice. Read his poems—it's only after shedding the inessentials that we might approach true living. He had conducted much of his difficult life, I would learn, by choosing the hard road leading to authenticity. He'd rarely held a job. He never had a car. He'd tramped about Italy staying in the cheapest *pensiones*. He'd survived homelessness, washing his socks in library bathrooms. He would type his poems on borrowed time at a friend's kitchen table.

When I asked about his health, there was a pause. "I don't want to get you in trouble," he said. He needed another moment to go on. He didn't have a phone, he explained, but it was as if the government could tap into his thinking, even without a phone. The voices. It was spoiling his ability to sleep. He was helpless. "It could be the government," he said.

Was there madness in him? Years earlier there had been an episode that had landed him at Danvers State Hospital for the Insane. It seemed present now; but there was genius in him too.

On September 5, 2014, Malcolm Miller lay unattended on the floor of that apartment, where empty bottles of Tylenol suggested that he had died in pain. I didn't know until I received a call from a city official to "come clear out his apartment because we have to open it up to the next tenant on the public housing list." Unbeknownst to me, I had been listed as Malcolm's emergency contact. During the year that I had known him, I had helped with occasional errands and, after persisting, had obtained his permission—he wrote it in a letter—to try to get his writing into print.

It was a lucky thing that I beat the city's clean-up crew to his place. I salvaged additional self-published books as well as typescripts of plays and novels, material that was headed for the trash. (That envelope stuffed with money? It went into probate and was eventually reclaimed by the state, after funeral home expenses were deducted.)

And so, as I began my retirement from teaching, I took up my work as friend and custodian of the writings of this poet. Some of his poems have now appeared in literary magazines. One won the poetry prize of the International Lawrence Durrell Society. Miller's books and papers have a permanent home in the Rare Books and Special Collections in the library of McGill University, where he earned a degree in 1954. He is the subject of the documentary film *Unburying Malcolm Miller* by Kevin Carey and Mark Hillringhouse.

Of Miller's 3500 or so poems, I have, with the help of the community of writers in Salem and the surrounding towns, culled the strongest and most vital, including those in this selection.

—Rod Kessler

# I Have Always Wanted

# What I Am Always Waiting For

I am always waiting for something
to happen that has never happened
I wake up in the ordinary way
and like you start by eating
and planning and hearing what
the earth is as it also wakes

by midmorning it overtakes my spirit
something I am always waiting for
something I cannot describe
I try to ward it off by beer
or wine at lunch
for it is like a great expectant joy
this awaited thing
but like a suffering more
harsh than winter

to no avail friendship
and sex and talk that stars
me as philosopher and wise man
to no avail for swift upon me
again it comes what I am always
waiting for
what I would welcome as a messiah
what I cannot describe
what has kept me sane and human
what makes me sorrow and sing

# Almost Free

once I was almost alive
almost human
almost free

once I almost saw
through eyes not merely me
in every light that ever dawned
I almost saw the world again

once I almost knew
the water that water is
in the river my both hands
gripped the wonder passing
to the sea

I was almost real
almost free

once I almost stood
in the immaculate morning
laughing with the sun
I was almost whole
almost alive

once there was a moment
not of time but endless
flowing now
I breathed it and was
almost the god
all secretly are and is

I was almost human once
almost free

# Free of Being Alive

while the cities sleep the great rivers
pour slowly through them
black with time
with the far-off hills

in the elaborate museums the expensive
masterworks remain on the walls
no eyes challenge the fortress
of their reputation

in beds marred by no waste
of finery the bodies of the most
beautiful women turn without
knowing they turn

free from disappointments
free from being alive
the dark long rivers glide
the water too is free

free of being anything
free of living anywhere
free of meaning anything

# The Dark Has Come

the dark has come
at the appropriate hour
to relieve the things
of this earth from
standing at attention

the dark has come
to let the grass rest
from the blinding sunlight
and the pebble to regain
the roots of its peaceful being there

from the darkening sky all the way
into the bones of animals
a message is being sent like music
that loosens the secret
fire to flow in our atoms as well as stars

# I Have Always Wanted

I have always wanted to get into
the growth of trees
to be half entangled in the upsurge
of branches
to lower myself to the darkness
of the roots and cool dark earth
beyond the enervating wilting sun of a wasteland

I have always wanted with women
to blaze at their breath
to grip every source of heat and skin
until I could not be sent
back to the world
without the rhythm of wind and fire
pulsing pulsing in their universal yes

I have always wanted something else
not people as they are
not life as they appear to live it
but to be even a murderer perhaps
covered in the blood of song
the murderer of their usual merely acceptable
selves in behalf of their greatest unslavery hour

# What Is That Sound

# Conquistador

to set out
of a morning and take
the first fresh light
on your sleep-dimmed skin

and reckon with the sea
banging out its call
for volunteers to taste
the cold tidal salt

to lure a careful
cat successfully to play
and feel the rich fur
and be hypnotized by its eyes

to drown in the general
drift of things
no more important than a tree
or a brick in a wall

to go from way to way
like a current of air
or a campfire story
told over and over

to gaze at the sky changing
and to know
in 10,000 years my kind
will be gazing gazing

and to come home baffled
by the wonder of things
to sit in your room
glowing like a star

# The Sea Doesn't Know

the sea doesn't know it's the sky
that makes it blue

nor does any day of the week mean
anything to time

I found at your mouth what you will never
find words for

nor need you find them
rivers do not choose which oceans

they enter but I touched something
in you that belongs to no one

# Rain

Something I can't say what
made me study rain
I walked in it
I watched it fall
I noted carefully
how one rain
differed from another
I took many photos
and filed many facts
and at last I came
to feel I knew
all about the rain
so I spoke out
I made my case
and people in the street
said there he is
the man who knows
all about the rain

but late last night
suddenly I woke
the rain was at my window
the day had been all clear
and bright
but in the dark the rain
came with wind
and woke me
and I lay alone
in the silent room hearing
the tap tap tap
like a secret code
and it was some time
after this I knew
without knowing why I knew
that I knew only
something of the rain
the rain knew
everything of me

# What Is That Sound

what is that sound I heard yesterday
it was like the sound
I heard the day before
and what is that sound
I am hearing now

coming across from the sea
and from the distant mountains
and across the plains
and through the streets of noisy cities
and the quiet towns of waiting

it is the song without ending
calling to no one
in particular
calling to no one
so everyone will hear

# In All Living Things

so it never be cursed
and enslaved with a name
so it never be discussed
in the House of Lords
and supplied to the people
like foul weather gear
or vitamins
so it baffle the gurus
whose antidotes
maim and corrupt
so it remain only possible
like a great fish
in the sea the sailor ponders
and seeks
so it not take the side
of the good
or the wicked
so it never be disabled
to neutrality and reasons

in all living things it has been
distributed as salt
in the vast waters
and wind in every portion
of endless blue

# Tonto

had more or less to
pretend to be flabber-
gasted by the white
man's prowess
what he really thought
of the Lone Ranger
we'll never know

Tonto who could track
the bad guys through
wasteland and canyon telling
by a hoofprint how
weary were the ponies
how many hours ago
they passed that way
Tonto who could scan
an arrow and without
blinking say apache or cherokee

understand me now I
have nothing against the Lone Ranger
I do not say he was
not a fighter for justice
in the old lawless west
but I inquire why he had
to wear a mask that's all
and why at the end of each
episode some jerk had to
stand hat in hand braying
son there goes
THE LONE RANGER!

why the huge fuss over
the great horse Silver
Tonto had a damned
fine pony too
and couldn't they have
mentioned even once Tonto
revered the Great Spirit

and felt the wonder of
lakes and mountains
and loved being alive

# The Taste of Inexplicable Nourishment

hitch-hiking days in the state of Maine
in the age of summer in the cold
sea winds of mid coast Maine the headlands
of rock so granite you would love
bitterly the raw bones of things
the rasp of brine in air wind-roughened

sleeping as best you could back of anybody's
town rolled up in a bag of duck feathers
and walking before dawn towards coffee
and donuts down some narrow road flaring
with pine trees' fragrance and into the darker
woods something like streams slipping
through and animals alive there with final stars

fading and wet slow kindly rain warmed
with Julyness like easy clean birth waking
and cleansing the drizzle hissing gently
in the trees and on the road involving
somehow everything of worthiness ever pertaining
to a young man being alive in the world

# A Clean Well-Lighted Place in Winter

it's 3 in the morning
the fatal lapsed hour
I am the sole
customer here
in this Dunkin Donut on
the coast of Massachusetts

the coffee is all right
the donut not bad
the music being offered
only fair
and behind the counter
the young woman
who quit high school
out of boredom
is yawning

a mute kind
of weary-eyed goddess

but a goddess none the less
in this god
blessedly open place
or don't you know
don't you know yet
about closed up towns
in cold dark times

# Regarding the Sky

the sky doesn't get
very tired
of being the sky

it doesn't know what
the sky is
the sky is very

lucky it doesn't
have to regret
a lapse of thunder

and lightning
even the most
electrifying and thunderous

or after a foot of snow suffer
an insufferable sense
of accomplishment

# Where Is Home

# Where Is Home

a bar of soap
running water and quiet
enough neighbors who can deal
with their own drives
where is home?
a chair a table from
anywhere they can
be grabbed
sleep on the floor as free
mysterious kings did
in the simpleness
of living things
where is home?
anywhere you can see a wide
spreading tree
sky that has no
prearranged master
where is home? ask a home
dwelling soul scrubbing
his floor with wide
flung windows hearing the Saturday
afternoon opera pausing
at a great aria to know
it's a lucky
man who finds a home

# My Mother Has to Go to the Rehab Hospital

I come to her old place
to pick up a few things
mail and the like and out
the window see
in the park under
the low hanging shade
trees a woman sitting
in a chair right where mother
used to sit

from this angle and distance it almost
is mother
but she will never sit under
the summer trees again
she is lying in the red
brick rehabilitation hospital
like a doll in its crib

she will never sit under
the summer trees again and the only
hope now is she
doesn't know it

# Piazza Santo Spirito

I remember waking up how cool
the villa floor was
Signora Pini brought the water in white pitchers
it was like a morning swim
washing so

how easy then to be a poem
at the window
they lowered baskets for the post
and raised them wondering like fishermen
what they had got

everything was like the wine
flaming red
the cheeses hanging in the shops
had the glow and value of pearls

standing with their feet turned out
the girls elegant as parasols
black olive eyes
and faces I recall making a bouquet

my evening grappa burned like hot white sun in me
and each step I took over the stones
had it seemed the imprint of some
permanent advance
so my mind closed down like school for the summer
and I acquired through sense
the purity of animals
within which I soon knew
how stupid we all were
with our pretense of living
how stupid we are still
though the world is a splendor

# The Day

the day spreads before me like an
ocean I may gaze upon
as waves tumble forward like children
somersaulting in a circus of their
own exuberance

I have nothing important to do
nothing worth getting disturbed
or inspired by

may this keep on forever
despite the stern helpful lectures
of competent people

# Waiting to Live

# Remarks Jotted Down While Waiting to Live

stupid people never know what to do with silence
and time but silence and time know very well
what to do with them

# I Am Waiting

one morning as they began
to give the sports results
over the airwaves
Yankees 4 Tigers 2 etc.
suddenly by some quirk
or other they began to give
the real results amid
swift protests and denials
despair 12 joy 2
propaganda 6 truth 1
piggishness 15 piety 1
suicides 3 resurrections 0

# State College Canteen

on his last day of work the guy
by some quirk of inspiration
profit or satire
loaded the huge soft
drink machines with beer
the price was right and the day
spring-like
never have students learned more
about religion
Dionysius was dancing in the halls
and singing in the corridors

never did the philosophy professor
a master of logical positivism
seem more absurd
his much-praised sobriety was found
to be a sort
of living death and all the English
instructors by afternoon were being
booed from the building
for not knowing how to teach
young people how to return
to the sun

# Growing Up

everyone gets born with two hands
you start off pretty much like others
it isn't easy to stand and run
the stars too are far off

you realize what a bird is
you follow it until it disappears as
you yourself will disappear
how much tedium is involved with shoelaces

you get the idea about grown ups
what is expected is neither falsity nor truth
you come to know why
when you hear Chinese or Arabic you're puzzled

for a while and then forget it
you forget your greatest moments too
but at funerals you succeed at solemnity
in the rain you carry an umbrella

if a god visits you, you keep
it to yourself

# Tourists

what have they come to see
so many hundreds of miles slowly
across droning repetitious highways
and inching traffic jams
steering evenly up to gasoline pumps
children smashing each other
with Kleenex boxes in the back seat

and to end up dressed undistinguishedly
in some inferior hotel with water
that barely goes down the basin
finding a twisted cigarette
butt and a condom in the drawer
later to trudge after a row of arrows
to gawk at a museum where cruel
people once killed harmless women

and the kids proudly wearing t
shirts with the city's name
rooked for too much money by smiling faces
the universal ice cream cones
jammed towards their mouths in exotic flavors

evenings wondering what to do next
missing home and the reassurance of custom
a kind of ordeal has them in its grip
days to go and almost every hour
money ebbs out of them like blood
from a wound
and the newness of the never seen
shining at times like something dreamed once
they don't always like
to wonder about again
having come so far to find
what is not really here anymore
or perhaps anywhere

# Meditations of Marcus Aurelius

The Caesar who abided many years
at the frontier of the Germans
did not miss the scented baths of Rome
or the piles of slave
produced exquisite fruit

by the dark forests year after year
he considered the sky a friend
he examined the existence of trees
and from birds heard
songs not meant for praise

he did not miss the urbane wits
sad like all socialites and sophisticates
or the trumpet-led processions
of superbly dressed clichés
but sat in his tent where nothing happened

at the core of things he felt
the void anyone feels
who does not care to make believe
that done he strapped on a sword
and civilized another mile

# Spring

the bars can no longer
hold these lost cowboys
full of beer and whisky
they stagger across the tree
still park
rained on by spring's need

careless of dark and puddle
they sing out and cavort
knocking trash barrels down
and adoring their souped
up getaway cars

when they break your sleep
at 3 a.m.
remember this
is the closest they might
ever get to joy
and freedom and god

# Yet I Am Truly Dead

I am dead already
here I stretch
out contentedly or not
dead dead as a door
nail except when you think
of it a nail has all those
atoms hopping and swaying in some
cosmic dance

yet I am dead truly here
gone gone to that other
side of things distant and buried
like a star in darkness

the whole town is out
of a Saturday night
drinking and thinking of what
to say next
I am stretched out here silently
accepting the night
of my own extinction
knowing what is beyond choice

the islands of Japan are floating
off the coast of Asia
huge slowly flapping birds
cross high green mountain valleys in Peru
the gold of the nation in banks
shimmers in clean solemn irrefutable stacks
I am dead here and poor as a pebble
the sea tide tosses aside casually
its happiness at being thus I envy

cars radio blasting varoom by
it is Saturday night to justify existence
in bars and cafes they try to be happy
hardworking people and not a demon among them
their time drips like an icicle
in the sunlight

stretched out as a bridge I lie
and death flows over me
then I head out alone like a road
at that hour when the world must sleep

# Côte-des-Neiges Cemetery, Montreal

a noble quiet is upon the wide
spread air row by row
I pause and read some stones
little is left of their pretenses and false hopes
their disappointments with human existence
they have been distilled down
to the last word
it is that word you must hear

I walk on one leaf-strewn path then another
in the vast fields people come to
when no choice is left
and I learn from below my feet
not to fear for they fear
nothing evil or good can mete out
purged of pettiness and boredom they do not need
your kindness or approval

some impeccable empowering dignity flows
out of how timelessly they lie there
faces steadfast to the sky
what they see or cannot see I gaze up to look for
and I seem to be proceeding over their accomplishment
step by step towards the green pastures
someone far away hears me singing
as if I am a rabbi who has found his way

# She Passed Through This Way

# The Sad Girl Who Sells Gasoline

the merit gas station on north
street in salem mass open
day and night in the dark hours
has a sad girl sitting
and waiting for you to come

drivers who drive in at 2 a.m. see
her sorrows as she sits
alone in her glass cage awaiting dawn
when she will rise and walk
away from so much gasoline

if you drive by wave at the sad girl
will you and smile as though yes
life is good it's all right
and if you need to fill your tank stop
there and tell her the gasoline is marvelous

# A Kind of Education

I loved a woman in that city
it was the end of winter
the snow lay embarrassed in the lanes
at its tenuousness
the trees stood around awkwardly

she was a woman of that city
it was not her way to speak of things
not her way to hear them out
she would walk faster when I spoke
of them her face buried

it was before spring we would
walk through the wet streets
when I was close something struck
like a great gong
through every bone and fiber of my blood

as long as I did not speak of things
like that
as long as I did not insist
who I am to her
the end of winter saw us together

under the grey sky
she safe in her silences
steering her even course
I a companion who had abandoned
all others for her

and I was right to do so
in love with a woman
who was the wrong woman
it was a kind of education in the beauty
and impossibility of things

# The Man Who Was Wrong but Right

a young Chinese woman with a beautiful
face stared at him
he followed her outside the cafe
into the street where she pointed
to something in the sky

he realized then she was not
pointing but trying to get a coat
sleeve more fully on

nor had she stared at him but merely sat
with a fixed gaze
she also was not Chinese but a white
eastern-looking woman possibly Jewish

you have been wrong in everything thus
far she murmured
but you are also right

an hour later in another section of the city
they entered her apartment

# Because of You, Woman of the North

I who do not go
to temples and synagogues
who is hardly in
the eyes of Jews
a Jew
who speaks no Hebrew
no Yiddish and feels
no special warming
glow amid my kind
in a few days as the days
of awe culminate I shall
be in a shul
amid a minion
for because of you my strength
is as the strength of ten

# Montreal Rue Victoria Near McGill

when we were just beginning remember
you said to get a strong
board to put under the mattress

the room was a little
bigger than the bed

over the everyday table I composed so
so poems on
a naked bulb testified
to the poverty
and marvel of human light

more than anything else but perhaps
some divinity your hips made
me eventually a poet

you've been lying up there 6
feet deep in a section
of your native town
almost 30 years
I am in love again

I am in love again and something
drew me to this street today
a huge aluminum looking office
building sits like a big tin can
where once that room defined
itself against the world as glorious

they have not improved
on that address
O still loved one

# She Passed Through This Way

she passed through this way
filling the air with being here
the dictionary began to flame
into a language of burning yes
tribes gathered with unheard of music

she stood there not allowed by usual conventions
the pebbles palpitated on the ground
the roots of trees went way down
as she breathed and branches burst
into poems she picked and ate

near her rain was superior
to sunshine elsewhere
she had come once before to pass through
no one who saw her would ever not see her
words spoken were washed in her silence to shining

# Susan

one less yes I will see
one less glow in the air
the stars in their blackness
have lost a golden glowing one

it has been 7 or 8 years since
those days I was awash
with the body of her ocean
that attained in each moment

the floodtide of some possible
her skin rich with smooth
strength sponsored a god
I have less god now

for I have become beset
by the dreaded words
of her death printed like shrapnel
pieces of her death will always pierce and grimace me

# Sex Goddess

please stop bursting without
warning upon me as I try to live
hundreds of miles away and am
not safe from the magnetism
under your skirts

why don't you stay in your own cell
why are you always like wind
borne pollen and I sneeze
sneeze until I am hospitalized
in Love Asylum and Bordello

how long can it go on the indifference
I feign at your genius
for delivering  me up to the stars
I am burning across the heavens
how can I earn a living worshipping life?

keep away from me please with the terrible
verdict that we love each other
can't we become sensible like others and die
to the glory of what your eyes offer
all my favorite people have become

so boring because of you
because of you I stop going to films
because of you I believe any miracle
including those I know cannot be real
because of you I ask the Mafia to protect me

# Poems Like This

# To Write

you will fail as a writer
until you encounter that
which is impossible to set down
but must be

# Poems Like This

I look at my hand descended
from knuckles that gripped
a much-bloodied club
my teeth have torn apart
wild beasts even those
of my own kind

my eyes are sullen unrelieved
by love or the tolerant kindness
of a healthy happy animal
my blood well-hidden in smooth
seeming tough skin and systems of
cordage and muscle yearns for
the evidence of life in
the blood of others

to look at me you would think
I was just another
person driving a car along
regulated roads or standing
patiently in line at the post
office supermarket or bank

you could have a congenial
enough drink with me at a bar
I could marry your favorite sister
or make you read
poems like this

# Baudelaire Lectures in Belgium to Raise Money

almost nobody
empty rowed tombstone chairs
in the voluminous hall his voice
a fly
trapped and bumping
on closed windows

a spider web
of silence fed
on his last hopes
last lost dreams
back to the city
of lights disheveled needing

a shave life
long dandy hatless now walking
blindly towards nowhere but hated
no one saw every
body was Baudelaire every
where was Belgium

# T. S. Eliot's First Wife

T. S. Eliot's first wife
weirdly lyrical with hesitant poetry
half-crazy in the dusk of evening
before dawn would gaze
her face the color of white
flame at the dying moon
he couldn't appease her strange destiny
what she yearned for he
stepped back from

# Blank White Page

something in the whiteness
though it shine with opportunity
something like a quality
of ominousness
something in that whiteness does
not want you

does not want your intelligent version
something in the whiteness has
its own shining white speechless god
lurking in the layers
of whiteness or something
remember when you lift your pen

above this whiteness a god dedicated
to it staying white watches
you with a dark regard
you can be washed off like a stain
like a mountain climber whose shriek
at the avalanches subsides

# What Happens to Promising Poets

what happens to them is what happens
to April and Christmas
presents and thousands of dollars

what happens to them is no one
is home when you knock and your voice
goes nowhere

what happens is a mountain
cannot be overcome by the eyes
and the terrible strong river

tumbling to the far ocean
waves will never care
what happens to them is what happens to everybody

# Middle-Aged Poet

coming back to a city of many years
I cannot telephone the death of my friends

at a hazy distance I glimpse them passing
in fine clothes with wives who know

all about yoga and oriental cooking
and how to enter and leave the real estate market

coming back to this city I cannot cry
out to them I have met along the ways

of nowhere the gods we stayed up all night
singing about

and heard the murmur of great things hidden
in the corners of words such as we hoped

I pass them by in the heart of downtown
and they stare straight ahead and step lively

as though I am a rather sorry rascal
who will ask for money or say a terrible thing

# Minor Poet Going into Business

last night I lifted the sun
from the sky screwing up
in its place a large watt bulb

this morning few knew the difference
and I have the sun
stretched out in my own mausoleum

if you know the difference
and want to see the sun lying in state
it will cost you a dollar

since there's still a moon
stars flowers birds and love
I plan to expand operations

having facsimiles for all
if you know the difference
and want to see the real stuffed and mounted

it will cost you a dollar
and I will make no exceptions
though major poets will be admitted free

once I devise facsimiles of them

# Among Human Things

# Offer

I am going to buy tomorrow
one of the new dictionaries on
sale that translates appearances
into reality
do you want me to
send you one

# Letter to an Old Girlfriend

I have a thousand
dollars in the bank
and an almost worthy hotel
room paid for a week

I am sitting here listening
to Bach on a little radio
smoking a cigar and drinking
a good European lager

the police or mafia are not
after me though
there was a chance they
could have been

outside is a small green park
sun is in the trees
and birds and you
you said I'd be a failure

# That Other Me

that other me keeps walking
I get tired or bored but he drags
me on through the spring bird songs
that other me
leaves big tips in restaurants
I say hey that's enough!
and that other me the BIG SHOT
throws down another dollar
and at my expense!

day after day and year after year
that other me is trouble
I say sensibly let it pass
what does it matter but that other me
like some silly John the Baptist cries
out the futile truth
that other me

and what a dolt with women that
other me selects the most
astounding ones!
I say choose more carefully learn
from experience but he
that other me just plunges on
with stupid hope while I am left
behind to clean up the mess

and I'm tired of it really
fed up with it and he knows
it and he laughs!
that other me I told him straight
out that's it goodbye
that other me
he's still around
can you believe it?
let us be absolutely candid
for a moment and tell
me how did you get rid
of that other you

# Another Country

I am spending some time
in another country
here time feels like it did before
it became time
here it seems not to break from the sky
into segments
from the sky that long ago told the sun here
is your home

I am spending some time here
in another country
and time remains
night falls but time does not
nothing it feels has really happened
to time from the beginning
it remains pure and endless
it cannot be determined by our
nervous necessities
it is just there like the sea
wave after wave

the most expensive watch cannot do
anything about it
compared to it everything else alive seems
some kind of slave

I am spending some time here
in another country
if you see me in your town looking
only like the others
like yourself it is because
I have had to return

# Employment Office Test

have you ever used a parachute
could you

do you believe a person can find more
eternity by contemplation and prayer

or by eating a certain diet like box
after box of strawberries

are you a loser who thinks he must die
or do you want to be frozen until paradise

if you had to be devoured by a beast which
beast lion elephant snake etc

you should have said sabre
toothed tiger for obvious reasons

you should not have said strawberries but stuck
to your principles

would you be willing to work for 7 dollars
an hour or 85 dollars a minute

consider that the latter could burn you
out fast and earn you less finally than the former

you should have jumped with a para-
chute when I pushed you too far

# Before the Nunnery

for some years I have been
passing here and gazing close
at the grey walls of well
quarried stone and fine trees beyond
now and then I've glimpsed clearly
a nun in her mysterious black

they might have sensed my strong gaze
they might have been aware it's always
me paying deep attention here
before they faded through many doors
down many corridors
silent with near invisibility

I am getting up my courage
I am going to cross the barrier
they will see me burst a door
and they'll scream and call the cops
or could they possibly murmur what
on earth took you so long

# Wall

civilizations pile up against it

great books almost are littered there

saints pulp-headed from hitting
their heads against it

every so often some genius or crack-
pot invents a way
through the wall

the victory song is hardly ended when it
seems another wall has grown up

the theory that walls are illusions
is paraded like a pet afghan
it wins a prize that entitles the owner
not to mention walls but to go around
the word with academic discretion

I make it through the wall today observing
my neighbor's wife bending over trying
to get the lawn mower started

# Among Human Things

among human things
are so many small
things we love unreasonably
and unseasonably
so many things no one
knows about we roll up
like rugs and old wool sox
so many things to be laid
neatly as flowers in a box
things intense as life
that mean we are

and things you can't
imagine nearly loving
eggbeaters for example
and pin cushions and hot
water bottles we store
in a drawer like intense
truths we will keep
like our teeth and hair

those ten bars of soap you
forgot in a cabinet how
joyously you unwrap them
out of curiosity years
later and look they look
like neat clean white
scrubbed farms glimpsed
from a train or highway

among human things if only
we could stop there gazing
at those clean white farms
or raincoats we have owned hanging
in closets that have known
so much darkness so many
instants of hope

# Fort Lauderdale, Florida

the sun here knows it has
no competition
it's the big shot that makes
you brown in a few days
you are mine the sun says
no one argues the point
which would require thought

civilization is not as real here
as the long sandy beach
where the amazing banality
of palm trees repeats itself like dogma
people look clean and light and fluffy
as if they have recently been sent
out to a laundry

# He Made It

from a high distant window in a well-packed library
on a snowy day in Canada
through a world of white I saw a man
running and running

for a large snow-clogged dim-windowed bus
that was a good ways ahead of him
and I could think only of this
watching and leaning forward in my chair

he didn't seem to have a chance out there
but he just made it
whereupon I unknown and unsuspected by him
sat humming and humming with the strange

gladness of the soul